sleepover scrapbook ™

Adapted by Marie T. Morreale

Based on the story and screenplay by Elisa Bell

SCHOLASTIC INC.

New York   Toronto   London   Auckland   Sydney
Mexico City   New Delhi   Hong Kong   Buenos Aires

ISBN 0-439-66058-0

™ & © 2004 Metro-Goldwyn-Mayer Studios, Inc. All rights reserved. Published by Scholastic Inc. SCHOLASTIC, and associated logos are trademarks and/or registered trademarks of Scholastic Inc.

Cover designed by Louise Bova
Interior designed by Louise Bova and Karen Hudson

12 11 10 9 8 7 6 5 4 3 2 1   4 5 6 7 8 9/0

Printed in the U.S.A.
First printing, September 2004

Roll Call!

Meet the Cast of *Sleepover*

Scavenger hunt! Julie, Hannah, Farrah, and Yancy vs. Molly, Jenna, Liz ,and Staci

Let's Get This Party Started!

Every 'tween and teen girl has been to a slumber party, but we bet very few guests have spent a night quite like the one in the movie *Sleepover*! MGM's *Sleepover* has food-fests, makeovers, gossip-jams, and a wild scavenger hunt where the winner wins the prized lunch spot.

On the following pages of this movie scrapbook you'll have an inside peek at the drama, giggles, and laughs that made this the sleepover to die for!

You're invited to a sleepover

School Daze! School's out! And it's summer fun for the Fielding Junior High grads. Parties, dates, beach days, and that night's sleepover party are the topics of conversation between Julie Corky and her best friend, Hannah. Silly String streaks by as kids throw their notebook paper to the wind. Even the girls' English teacher, Mr.

Julie and Hannah check out Mr. Corrado's reading list.

Corrado, can't spoil the mood as he hands out a summer reading list.

But all thoughts of the book list fade away as Julie and Hannah's friend Farrah rushes over with news that there's a party problem—the school's reigning teen queens are having a sleepover on the same night. Farrah pulls out the evidence: a bright orange, Popsicle-shaped invitation that reads "Liz's Slumber Blowout."

And that means Staci Holden, the most popular girl in school, will be going to her best friend Liz's house and *not* Julie's.

Just then Staci and Liz pass by as Julie, Hannah, and Farrah are joined by Yancy. The teen queens stop for a moment and insult Yancy about her weight. Then they glide away

Julie and Hannah are ready for summer.

to once again reign over their own little world.

Julie sees the hurt on Yancy's face and, trying to fix things, asks her to join her slumber party that night. Yancy agrees, and all is well until the girls are knocked over by Russell Alterman, the ultimate skateboard geek— unkempt hair, blue braces, wristbands up his arms, big shorts, and all.

Russell overhears Julie and her friends talking about the sleepover, and he grabs an invitation.

"Par-tay at Julie's!" he oozes.

"Don't even," Julie warns, hoping that Russell and his skateboard buddies will stay away, far away.

Not only does Julie *not* want to deal with Russell and his silly pals, but she wants to spend some fun, quality time with Hannah, who is moving away with her family later that summer. Not only will Julie miss Hannah terribly, but she dreads the thought of starting high school without her best friend.

As they walk home, Julie and Hannah pass by the high school's campus, and they glance over at the fabled fountain—where the really cool kids hang out. "There it is," says Hannah. Even now, on the last day of school, the fountain is populated with guys in lettermen jackets and perky girls showing off their cheerleader outfits and moves. Across from the fountain are tables next to the dumpsters. That's where the wannabes and geeks gather.

"And that's where I'll be sitting," Julie moans.

All of a sudden, Steve Phillips, the ultimate cool skateboarder, zooms by on his board and soars over and across the fountain! Julie's heart begins to pound because she has a major crush on Steve.

The fountain—the ultimate high school cool spot.
Steve Phillips glides over it on his skateboard.

As Julie and Hannah continue on, they pass one of the popular high school hangouts, Robek's. The screech of tires distracts them, and they turn to see Staci sitting next to her boyfriend, Todd, in his convertible. He's a quarterback on the high school football team. As Todd stops the car next to Julie and Hannah, Staci leans over.

"Jules, can't make your overnighter," she says triumphantly. "I'm doing the dance with Todd. . . . The *high school* dance."

As they zoom off, Julie wonders how and when things changed so drastically. She and Staci used to be great friends. But that was in elementary school.

Staci and Todd zoom by in his convertible.

The Home Front

Things at school may have changed, but as Julie and Hannah entered the Corkys' house, they realized that some things stay the same.

Julie's mom Gabby was preparing for the night's sleepover. She was vacuuming, fluffing pillows, and dusting.

"There are a million things that need to get done before the party, Julie," her mom said. "So I stopped on the way home and bought all the stuff."

Much to Julie's horror, "the stuff" was spilling out of a Party Playhouse shopping bag: a ladybug piñata, ladybug antennae headbands, ladybug coin purses, and ladybug socks.

"Mom. *Hello*. I'm fourteen. Not four," Julie insists.

Julie's mom is all set for the party.

As her mom puts on ladybug antennae to show them what fun a theme party would be, Julie's scruffy older brother, Ren, wanders into the room. Ren had dropped out of college and moved back home so he could "find himself." So far the only thing he had found was the box of Krispy Kremes in the kitchen.

Thankfully, the ladybug theme was soon forgotten, and Julie's mom explained that she had planned on going out with her girlfriends, leaving Julie's dad at home to look after the party.

"No leaving the house. No boys. No damaging important stuff," Julie's mom warned.

Party, Party!

Everything is ready for the sleepover. Julie and Hannah are putting the finishing touches on the food menu: fried Twinkies. Julie's dad pops a Twinkie in his mouth and gives Julie a thumbs-up. For a moment, Julie's mom has second thoughts about going out. Julie's dad would be busy installing a water-purifying system in the kitchen, and Ren, well, Ren was just *Ren*!

Could the girls manage on their own? But Julie and Hannah shoo her out the door and assure her that everything will be fine.

Mmmm! Julie and Hannah fry up some Twinkies for the party.

Hannah, Farrah, and Yancy raid the closet to create their own fashion looks.

When Farrah and Yancy arrive, the girls head to Julie's bedroom and get in the party mode. They turn up the music and are ready to p-a-r-t-y. It's time to experiment with makeup, clothes, hair color, and Presto Tan in a can!

Farrah, Yancy, and Hannah check out Julie.

Farrah likes her mod look.

Meanwhile . . .

Staci, who has passed on Liz's slumber party to go out with her boyfriend, Todd, is dressed to kill. After all, she's going to a high school dance. But when she hops into Todd's car, Staci notices that he is wearing jeans and a T-shirt—hardly dance attire.

"I thought the dance was semiformal," Staci asks Todd.

"We're skipping the dance," Todd replies as he peels out of her driveway.

A few minutes later, as Staci is fuming, Todd pulls into a dimly lit park. He's decided that instead of going to the dance, they are going to spend some private one-on-one time. Staci doesn't *think* so and storms out of the car.

"Have you forgotten who I am?" Todd snarls as Staci slams the car door.

PatrolTec security guard Sherman is on the lookout for trouble at the Corky house.

"Let me think," she says sarcastically. "The *second-string* quarterback? On the *junior varsity*!"

As an angry Todd tears off, Staci looks around and realizes she is near Julie's house. That's when a lightbulb goes off in her head and she pulls out her cell phone to call Liz.

Staci heads for Julie's house after she leaves Todd.

"Liz, change of plan. I can't get you guys into the dance. Calm yourself. I have a new funness in mind. Start making a list," Staci coos as she heads for Julie's house.

Julie and the gang are ordering pizzas when the doorbell rings. They rush to answer it. And there, standing before them, is Officer Sherman Shiner—PatrolTec security guard. He is checking on the loud music and warns them to keep it down. The girls giggle when he leaves. Quiet—yeah, right!

Back at Party Central

"**T**urn up the music!" Hannah says. The girls are having a blast. At that moment, there's a knock at the door. Julie opens it, expecting Sherman to be back. The girls are shocked to see Staci standing there. Staci explains that she and Todd had taken care of business and decided to pass on the dance.

"Let's get this gala started," Staci says as she heads toward Julie's bedroom. "What's your e-mail?" Staci asks.

"FlatGal at AOL," Julie says, a bit embarrassed.

Snickering, Staci calls Liz on the phone and explains that she has cooked up some fun for the evening: competing scavenger hunts for Julie's partygoers and Liz's guests.

Staci has big plans for the two sleepovers—a scavenger hunt!

At Staci's instructions, Julie switches on her webcam, and Liz, Jenna, and Molly appear on the computer screen.

Minutes later, Staci prints out an e-mail from Liz. It's the scavenger hunt list.

Each sleepover group must get all the items on the list, and the first group to show up at the high school parking lot that night wins. The winner gets the prized fountain lunch spot at the high school next year.

Julie nearly faints! Not only is the scavenger hunt totally against her mom's "house rules," but getting Steve Phillips's—her secret crush—boxer shorts—no way!

Julie and Hannah check out the scavenger hunt list.

Nervous, Julie wonders how they can possibly sneak out of the house. But Hannah has the answer to that—Ren! Of course, it will take cold, hard cash. Julie will pay him fifty dollars so he can cover for them.

As Julie and Hannah finish their negotiations with Ren, they find Staci in an e-mail conversation with someone. It's a guy from DatesSafe.com named Dave, and Staci's arranging for Julie to meet him at the Cosmo Club at nine o'clock that night. She describes Julie as a twenty-five-year-old swimsuit model named June and mentions that he can recognize her because she'll be wearing a purple scarf. Julie will recognize her date, Dave, by his brown jacket. Just as Staci confirms the date, she's beeped. It's Liz. She and Jenna and Molly are outside in her Beemer ready to pick her up. Liz, who stayed behind one year in school, is old enough to have her learner's permit.

"You didn't for serious think I was going to be on *your* team, did you?" Staci says sarcastically as she leaves.

✳ Have a guy from DatesSafe.com buy you a soda at the Cosmo club. Take a Polaroid photo.

Dress Up— Sneak Out!

As Hannah and Farrah work fashion magic on a sparkly red cocktail dress from Julie's mom's closet, Julie begins to have an anxiety attack. With each rip and pull on the dress, Julie gets worse. Even the finishing touch of her mom's purple scarf doesn't help. How is *she* going to look like a twenty-five-year-old swimsuit model? How are *they* going to get to the Cosmo Club? she wonders.

Julie tries on one of Mom's cocktail dresses.

Within minutes, all problems are solved. The girls have tranformed Julie into a sophisticated dream girl. Yancy has figured out where she can get a car. And Ren has his eye on Dad, who is under the sink in the kitchen working on the purifying system. All they have to do is get out of the house without being seen!

Julie is all dressed up.

Out the window and onto the arbor.

The girls decide to climb out onto the arbor that stands outside Julie's window. They all make it unscathed—except Julie, whose high heel gets stuck. As she pulls it free, she falls through the arbor and dangles head-first in front of the kitchen window, right where her dad is working! Luckily, he's too absorbed in his plumbing to notice his daughter and her friends. They take off for Yancy's house to pick up her father's green electric car.

Julie gets stuck.

Whatta predicament for Julie!

"Officially. The smallest car I've *ever* seen," Julie says as Yancy pulls up to the garage door.

"It looks like a clown car," Hannah adds.

"It's an English car, so the steering wheel is on the right-hand side." She assures them that her dad taught her how to drive it—in the Wal-Mart parking lot. Since the car is really a two-seater, Julie, Hannah, Yancy, and Farrah squeeze in. Oomph—finally, they get the door closed!

The girls wonder how they will ever get into Yancy's electric car!

They squeeze in!

The UninVited

Only seconds after Julie and her friends have left her house, Russell and his skateboard buddies, Lance and Miles, arrive. They are wearing headset communication devices and zoom over Julie's yard on their skateboards. They climb up the arbor, which is damaged from the girls' escape, and end up spilling into Ren's room. Soon they find Julie's room but no girls, so they begin to snoop around. As they search for Julie's diary, Russell suddenly falls. Julie's dad calls out, "Girls? Everything all right up there?"

As he heads up to make sure, the Spice Girls' "Tell Me What You Want" blares from Julie's room. Julie's dad opens the bedroom door,

Lance, Miles, Ren, and Russell decked out in wigs and robes.

Russell discovers the scavenger hunt list.

and looks inside. He sees four girls in robes dancing to the music. Now if he looked from another angle, he would have seen Russell, Lance, Miles, and Ren all dressed up in wigs, scarves, and the girls' bathrobes!

When Julie's dad sees everything is okay, he goes back downstairs, and the guys quickly pull off their costumes. Russell spies Julie's computer and the scavenger hunt list. It's time to go!

Number One on the List!

As Julie and her friends arrive at the mall, they spot Staci, Liz, Jenna, and Molly leaving Old Navy. Staci is holding a Polaroid snapshot of the mannequin in the window, which is now wearing the outfit Staci wore to school that day.

"Good luck," Liz says smugly as they pass each other.

Ignoring the jibe, the girls head into the store. It's just about to close, so they have to hurry. The first window is locked. They find one that is open—it has a male mannequin. As they try to dress the mannequin his arm falls off. It's a disaster—and a worse one when Sherman, the PatrolTec guard, passes by the window.

"Freeze!" Julie hisses to the girls. And all four of them stop in midair. When Sherman turns away, they go back to dressing the mannequin. And every time Sherman turns around, they freeze in position. Finally finished, Hannah gets ready to take the Polaroid proof. But Sherman turns around again and sees them. Furious, he charges into the store after them, but the girls escape and are off to the next item on the list: the Cosmo Club.

* Dress a window mannequin in your clothes at Old Navy in the mall. Take a Polaroid photo.

Hannah and Farrah try to dress the male mannequin in the Old Navy window.

With a little teamwork they get the job done.

Pizza Time

The girls pile back into Yancy's car, but back at Julie's house the pizza delivery guy is dropping off the five pies they had ordered. Julie's dad pays for the pizza and starts to walk upstairs to Julie's room. Luckily, Ren appears in the hallway and offers to deliver the pizzas

Julie calls Ren and tells him he has to eat all the pizzas!

to the girls. Although Julie's dad thinks it's weird that Ren is being so helpful to Julie and her friends, he's more concerned about his Aquapurefilter system back in the kitchen. He hands the pizza over to his son.

As if on cue, Ren's cell phone rings. It's Julie asking if the pizzas have arrived. When Ren tells her yes, she tells him he has "to make them all disappear!"

Being the good big brother—and with the offer of Julie doing his laundry for a month—Ren and the family dog start to scoff down the pizzas. They have a long way to go.

Even the family dog is in on the plan!

The Cosmo Club

Julie, Hannah, Yancy, and Farrah arrive at the Cosmo Club, only to run into Russell, Miles, and Lance. The bouncer takes a good look at the ragtag team and turns them away. Discouraged, they all plop down on the curb and try to figure out how to sneak in.

Just then, the DJ's van pulls up and the gang sees their way in—the huge speaker boxes! A perfect hiding place for Julie and Hannah! Once in the back door of the Cosmo Club, the girls pop out of the boxes and head toward the sound of the music.

Julie and Hannah sneak into the club in a speaker box.

Neon dance floor. Swirling lights. Wall-to-wall people.

"Look at this place!" Julie says excitedly.

"It rocks!" Hannah agrees.

But there's no time to enjoy the scene. The girls have to hurry to find Julie's date. Julie and Hannah spy Staci and Liz, who are about to get their picture taken with a guy buying them a drink.

"We have to find Dave," Hannah says.

Just then, Julie spies their junior high English teacher, Mr. Corrado! And he's wearing a brown jacket.

"Mr. Corrado is my *date*!" Julie wails. "We have to get out of here! He'll report us for sure!"

Staci thinks her team will win.

As Julie and Hannah try to make their way *away* from Mr. Corrado, they push through the crowd. But Mr. Corrado has spied the telltale purple scarf and heads toward Julie.

"June?" he calls out, as Hannah hides behind a plant.

Julie turns toward Mr. Corrado. She pulls down her sunglasses and tries to be a cool twenty-five-year-old swimsuit model. It works—at least for a while. Mr. Corrado doesn't recognize Julie and leads her over to get a drink. But when the bartender asks to see her ID, Mr. Corrado finally realizes that his date is none other than Julie Corky!

Defeated, Julie quickly explains the situation. Amazingly enough, Mr. Corrado understands. He went to Abbott High School and admits he *never* got to sit at the fountain for lunch. He agrees to have Hannah take a photo of him with Julie holding a drink—a ginger ale with olives! The girls are ecstatic.

Outside, by the backstage door, Farrah and Yancy are waiting for their friends. Farrah decides to get a cup of coffee and leaves Yancy alone. But she's not alone for long. The cute guy who had helped deliver the speakers comes out of the stage door and starts talking to her. And he's flirting with her! Yancy is amazed.

His name is Peter, but he can't hang out—he's got another gig to go to. So when Farrah returns with her coffee, he splits, but Yancy is in seventh heaven! Until they bump into Staci and her friends. Of course, something like Staci and her rat pack will bring anyone back down.

"Your girls are drinking with Mr. Corrado," Liz hisses.

"Total grode!" giggles Jenna.

"Pa-the-tic!" adds Staci.

Julie's DatesSafe.com date—is Mr. Corrado!

Hannah snaps Julie's scavenger hunt photo with her date.

✳ Have a guy from DatesSafe.com buy you a soda at the Cosmo Club. Take a Polaroid photo.

Exit . . . the Cosmo Club

Julie's mom shakes it up on the dance floor.

"**I** think I just had a stroke!" Julie whispers to Hannah as they start to leave the club.

But as they head out, Julie notices a group of "older" women dancing, and one of them looks familiar. Julie takes a closer look and notices that right in the middle is her MOM!

"What is she doing?" Julie exclaims. "She isn't supposed to—wiggle—that way. She's a mother. She uses Saran Wrap. She makes mac and cheese. And drives a Volvo!"

Julie and Hannah have to get out of there quickly because Julie's mom seems to be headed their way. As they flee, the purple scarf slips off Julie's neck, and seconds later, Julie's mom nearly trips on it.

She recognizes it. As she looks through the crowd, she notices a figure walking out the door. Is it Julie?

Julie's mom rushes outside but doesn't find her daughter.

Little does she know that Julie, Hannah, Yancy, and Farrah have hidden in a dumpster. As they peek out, Julie sees that her mom is trying to make a phone call.

"I'm beyond dead. She's calling Dad!" Julie says.

Luckily for Julie, her mom is unable to get clear reception on her cell phone.

The girls hide in a dumpster.

Julie's mom calls home from the Cosmo Club.

So Julie's mom heads back inside to use the pay phone in the ladies' room. Julie begins to panic. She *has* to get home before her mom calls! Oh, no! As the girls exit the dumpster they notice that a huge delivery truck has blocked Yancy's car. Just when things couldn't get any worse, Russell skates up and asks, "Where to next?"

Without missing a beat, Julie slips out of her high heels, hooks them in her ribbon belt, jumps on Russell's skateboard, and skates off. Hair flying in the wind, Julie leapfrogs over a dog, grabs hold of the back of a truck, and almost crashes into a car driven by two guys.

"Who is that girl?" the driver asks, impressed by Julie's skateboarding skills.

Who was that guy? Little does Julie know it was her dream-hunk, Steve Phillips, with his best bud, Gregg.

Safe at home, she flies off the board. Realizing she can't climb up the broken arbor, she looks for a way in. Just then she hears her dad pick up the ringing phone. It's Mom!

As her dad starts to call for Julie, it's Ren to the rescue. He turns on the water faucet his dad has been "working" on. And just as Ren expected, a water geyser shoots up. What a disaster! Julie's dad drops

Julie is on a mad dash back home.

the phone and runs to hold back the floods. Julie sneaks in!

Julie's dad manages to pick up the phone and hears Julie's mom saying sternly, "Put Julie on the phone."

In the nick of time, Julie throws on a robe over her dress and takes the phone from her dad. Disaster evaded!

Back to the Hunt

The scavenger hunt isn't over. Julie thinks there's still time to catch up with Staci's gang. Yancy and the girls have unblocked the car and are waiting for Julie outside her house. She squeezes in and they head for Steve Phillips's house. But just as they pull up in front of his house, the electric car loses power.

Hannah tells Julie to go get the boxer shorts and they will fix the car.

Julie doesn't want to go into Steve's house. She might run into him as she steals his boxers. But it has to be done.

As Julie sneaks through the sliding glass doors at the rear of Steve's house, Staci and Liz see her. Staci grabs her cell phone and dials the PatrolTec Security number.

Julie hides under the pool table in Steve's rec room.

"I'd like to report a suspicious person," Staci tells the operator. Staci and her friends have already found Steve's boxers in the back-seat of his car.

Julie's in Steve's kitchen where she sees his skateboard lying on the kitchen table. The Holy Grail! As she reaches out to touch it, she hears Steve and his friend Gregg talking about some girl. Julie quickly tries to escape into a room down the hall and she nearly bumps into Steve. But he is too busy concentrating on his old Fielding Junior High yearbook. He's trying to identify the girl they saw skateboarding earlier. Julie sneaks into the bathroom and hides in the shower.

"I think I recognize her from somewhere. I think I knew her in, like, grade school or something," Steve says to Gregg as he points out a picture.

Julie stretches from her hiding place in the shower to hear what they are saying. Did Steve actually say *her* name? As she leans forward to hear better, she almost runs straight into Steve's hand. He turns on the water so he can take a quick shower before the dance. And there's no place to hide!

Steve and Gregg see what the loud noise is on the lawn.

Just as Steve is about to step in the shower, he hears a strange noise out on his lawn. It sounds like a car crash.

Steve wraps a towel around his waist and runs to see what's going on. Julie makes her escape, only to quickly double back to grab Steve's abandoned boxers on the bathroom floor.

"What the heck was that noise?" Steve asks Gregg.

They peer out the window and see an empty tiny green car smashed into a PatrolTec car. Yancy had found an electrical outlet on Steve's lawn. But once the car got enough juice, it started on its own and ran right into Sherman's patrol car.

As Julie scurries around the side of Steve's house, she hears a booming voice say: "Halt!" It's Sherman, and Julie's been spotted.

Down the street, Staci, Liz, Molly, and Jenna are sitting in the Beemer watching the whole scene unfold.

"And . . . we win," Staci says as they all high-five each other. Staci mentions that they don't have to hurry to the high school since Julie has a "date" with Sherman. She suggests that they stop for a celebratory juicer.

But this makes Liz suspicious.

"Is there a *reason* you don't want to go to the dance?" Liz asks. "Like a *Todd* reason?"

The Long Arm of the Law

Sherman shines his flashlight right in Julie's eyes. He thinks he recognizes her, but he can't quite place this drenched teenager. He marches Julie to his car, but when they get there, the green minicar is gone.

Sherman wonders what happened to it, but he's more concerned about bringing Julie to justice. Julie figures she's caught, so she tells him her name and phone number, and Sherman dials it on his cell phone. Feeling beat, Julie listens as Sherman speaks to her father.

"Your father wants to speak to you," Sherman says as he hands the phone to Julie.

Julie's dad is still trying to install the water purifier.

Petrified, Julie takes the phone and whispers, "Dad?"

"Fifty monthly," Ren says. "For six months!" It's Ren! He and the family dog have the girls' shoes on and have been making a racket so her dad thinks everything is fine.

Once again her brother has saved the day. And he's not the only one. As Julie hands Sherman back the cell phone, Yancy and the girls push pedal to metal in the little green car and pull Julie in. Unfortunately, Sherman can't follow because when he was calling Julie's dad, Russell had sneaked up and let the air out of his tires.

Before Julie heads off, she reaches out and grabs the PatrolTec decal off the side of Sherman's car. Oh, yeah. They've won the scavenger hunt!

The family dog is ready to party!

Never Say Die!

As the girls' car speeds by the Robek's, they see Staci and her pals coming out with juicers in hand. Staci and her friends look pretty smug and satisfied until they notice Yancy's car heading to the high school.

The juicer gals scramble to Liz's BMW and step on it. The chase is on. The two cars race to the high school parking lot at the same time!

Julie and Staci both get out of the car. They pull out the scavenger hunt items: Steve's boxer shorts, the photo from the Old Navy window, the photo at the Cosmo Club, and the PatrolTec decal.

* Get a security decal off the ParolTec car.

"Tie!" Julie says.

"We share the spot," Hannah says.

"Share?" says Staci incredulously. "With you? Don't think so. Tiebreaker. Winner takes all."

Liz steps up and says, "The first one to get the king or queen's crown at the dance wins."

That decided, Jenna notices Todd's car in the parking lot.

"I thought you said you guys decided to skip the dance, Staci," Jenna says a bit cattily.

Staci huffs off toward the high school gym and the girls follow, eager to see what's going on.

* Get Crown

Staci and her crew celebrate with juicers . . . only to see the
green car pass by them, heading toward the high school.

Julie and her friends are determined to get into the dance, too. Just then, Russell skates
up, still laughing about Sherman and his pancake-tired car. Julie quickly explains that there
is a tiebreaker and now they have to get the crown.

Russell pulls out his scavenger hunt list and adds, "Crown."

A Night to Remember

Staci and her friends have managed to get into the dance. So when Julie and her friends get to the entrance, she doesn't let the lack of tickets stop them. Julie convinces the girl at the door to let them in.

The first thing they notice in the gym is a giant banner: A NIGHT TO REMEMBER. It's decorated with Mylar moon balloons, shiny streamers that look like rain, and a papier-mâché forest of trees. The strobe lights flash as kids dance to a live band. It's everything Julie dreamed it would be!

Staci and the girls see Todd kissing another girl!

Julie and Hannah start to scope out the crowd to see if they can find Steve. On the other side of the room, Staci asks Liz if she has seen Scott.

"Not yet," Liz says. "Remain calm until the evidence is in."

Though neither Julie nor Staci spots the object of her affection, both Steve and Todd are at the dance.

Steve is trying to still identify the girl he saw on the skateboard and asks friends if they remember a girl named Julie Corky. A cute girl comes over to Steve and asks him to

Julie and the gang rock out.

dance. Though he's more interested in finding out about the blur in red on a skateboard, he doesn't want to hurt the girl's feelings and heads to the dance floor with her.

Julie sees them and her heart sinks. Ever the best friend, Hannah says a bit lamely, "Maybe they just met."

Maybe. But just as Julie is about to think the absolute worse, Farrah pops up. Alert! Todd is kissing some girl in the "forest," and it's *not* Staci. As a matter of fact, Staci is heading straight for them! The girls race over to check out the scene.

"Guess you changed your mind," Staci says to Scott. "About the dance."

A surprised Scott spins around toward Staci, and she *slaps* him! The girl with Scott turns out to be Linda—his *girl-friend* of six months! Before anyone can stop

Staci lands on the floor.

them, Linda and Staci begin pushing each other and really getting into it. Papier-mâché trees are falling over like they were in a logging camp. Linda shoves Staci really hard, and she lands on a big fake rock and she can't get out of it. Embarrassed and hurt, Staci is helped up by Liz as Todd and Linda walk away together.

But it's Russell who really heals Staci's fragile ego.

"If I had a girl like Staci, I'd worship her," Russell tells Todd.

The dance contest is about to begin, and Linda urges Todd to enter with her. Over her shoulder, she says to Staci, "Too bad. So sad. Guess you don't have anyone to enter with."

Never to be defeated, Staci grabs Russell's hand and spits back, "Oh, yes, I do!"

Everyone heads to the dance floor. Julie, Hannah, Yancy, and Farrah are all dancing together, while Todd and Linda can't really dance to the beat. But Russell, the stumbling skateboarder, turns out to be on fire on the dance floor, and he and Staci are making quite a scene. As he busts a major move, a piece of paper falls out of his back pocket. Steve, who is standing by watching, picks it up and reads it.

It's the scavenger hunt list! And Julie's name is on it next to "Get Steve's boxer shorts."

Everything begins to make sense to Steve. Gregg points out something on the dance floor. "Dude. Look, the girl in the red dress!" he says.

Steve looks over and sees Julie and smiles. He knows what he's going to do next.

Just then, the winners of the dance contest are announced. It's Staci and Russell. And Russell is in heaven.

Steve finds Russell's scavenger hunt list.

More Miracles!

While Russell and Staci find romance in the air, Yancy is not to be left out. The band's singer steps up to the microphone. It's time to announce the king and queen of the dance. But first, he has a special dedication.

"To Yancy. From the speaker movin' guy!" the singer croons into the microphone.

Yancy freezes in her tracks and is eye to eye with Peter, the cute guy she met at the Cosmo Club.

"Told you I had another gig," Peter explains. "Saw you dancing out there. Wanna try a partner?"

As Julie and Hannah see their friend glide away, they are happy for her. But Julie admits her heart is still breaking.

"Julie?" Steve calls from the stage.

"Someone for everyone," she whispers. "Except me."

Hannah tries to lift Julie's spirits and suggests they try to find the king or queen's crown and win the scavenger hunt. Julie, Hannah, and Farrah head backstage, but all they find is Liz, Molly, and Jenna.

Once again the band's singer goes to the microphone. He's ready to reveal the king and queen.

"Jennifer Allen and Steve Phillips!" he announces.

Julie's heart leaps and almost crashes when Liz confidently says that Jennifer Allen is a friend of hers and will definitely give them her crown. So they will win!

Steve and Jennifer are crowned to the cheers of the crowd.

"Choose your partners," the singer tells Steve and Jennifer. "This song is reserved for you."

Jennifer heads straight for her boyfriend, but Steve steps up to the microphone and calls out, "Julie?"

Hannah pushes Julie right in front of Steve, and he reaches out and asks, "Wanna dance?"

Unable to speak, Julie nods and falls into his arms. Finally, she finds her voice and tells him she didn't know he even knew who she was. Instead of answering her, Steve smiles and places his crown on Julie's head.

"You win," he says. After all, he had found Russell's scavenger hunt list and knew what would clinch the contest.

Seeing this, Hannah, Yancy, and Farrah scream in unison, "We win!" And Liz, Jenna, and Molly all turn on Staci and say, "It's all *your* fault!"

After the dance, Julie and Steve walk hand in hand over to the infamous fountain. He starts to explain that he saw her on the skateboard earlier that night and then found out about the scavenger hunt. Just as Steve leans to kiss her, Julie's cell phone rings.

It's a Ren-alert. Mom is on her way home. She and the girls have to get back to the house. "I have to go!" she says to Steve, and leaves him in her dust.

Julie's dream dance with Steve.

"We have to get back to the house," the girls tell Julie.

It's a race to the Corky house. The girls in the green car pull up beside Julie's mom's Volvo. Just as they are trying to outrun Gabby, PatrolTec Sherman pulls up behind them—on a bicycle. When he sees who's in front, he starts to pedal after them, but Julie's crown has flown out of the car and punctures the bike tire.

"That's it!" Sherman moans. "I'm going back to work at the Krispy Kreme."

By seconds, the girls beat Julie's mom to the house. They spill out of the car, and Julie shows them Ren's old abandoned fort. It's fifteen feet from her window. Julie calls out to Ren and he appears in her window as she scrambles to the top of the fort. She throws him a rope to hold tightly. Julie has the girls shinny across the rope to the window just as her mom's car pulls in the driveway.

Ren pulls the rope too tight and pulls over the fort. Hannah, Farrah, and Yancy can literally walk in the window, but Julie is back on the ground! She

Sherman never gives up!

has to try to slip in the side door without anyone seeing her. While her dad has led her mom into the kitchen to taste his newly purified water, Julie sneaks in.

Julie creeps into the bedroom, and the girls heave a sigh of relief and climb into their sleeping bags.

The next morning, Julie's dad calls them down for pancakes. He mentions that the old fort collapsed last night. Changing the subject quickly, Ren reveals he's decided to go back to college.

"Thinking I might have a career ahead in surveillance," he says, winking at Julie and the girls.

When Julie's mom asks how everything went the night before, Julie has a moment of conscience and after a few uncomfortable moments, she confesses, "We left the house. . . . But I assure you, it was for a very important adolescent cause."

Instead of an explosion, Julie's mom says that she understands that Julie is growing up. "Just take your time," she advises as she hugs Julie.

After Yancy and Farrah take off, Julie says good-bye to Hannah. When she goes back to

A mother-daughter moment.

A perfect kiss!

her bedroom, she plops on her bed and looks out over the ruins of the fort. But something shiny in the fort window catches her eye. It's her crown!

Julie climbs out her window onto the fort. She reaches for the partially crushed crown and a hand appears. It's Steve's, and he takes the crown and places it on Julie's head. And without a moment's hesitation, he leans over and kisses Julie.

Life is perfect!